I Belong to:

_____

If found, please return to:

_____

_____

_____

Speak Life poetry

Supernatural Poetic Expressions of Anointed Knowledge

Volume 1: Identity

Mission:

*Confidently Knowing who
YOU are IN Christ Jesus!*

LAKANJALA K. WILLIAMS

Heavenly
Light Press

Alpharetta, GA

Holy Bible, New Living Translation, copyright © 1996, 2004, 2015 by Tyndale House Foundation. All rights reserved.

Scripture quotations from The Authorized (King James) Version. Rights in the Authorized Version in the United Kingdom are vested in the Crown. Reproduced by permission of the Crown's patentee, Cambridge University Press

"Scripture quotations taken from the Amplified® Bible (AMP), Copyright © 2015 by The Lockman Foundation. Used by permission. www.lockman.org"

ISBN: 978-1-6653-0570-9

Credits:

Book Cover and "Sister Girls" Illustration:
Damon Danielson of Divine Image Graphics, Inc.
Book Editor 1: Suzanne Mohr
Book Editor 2, Interior Design: Keilah Johnson of Row Branding, LLC
Publisher: Heavenly Light Press, an imprint of BookLogix

THIS BOOK IS DEDICATED TO

MY SON DILLON,
MY DAUGHTERS LILLIAN AND LEILANI,
ALL OF MY COUSINS,
HONORARY DAUGHTERS,
AND ALL THE WOMEN AND LITTLE GIRLS
ALL OVER THE WORLD.

I WANT YOU ALL TO KNOW THAT
NO MATTER HOW MANY OBSTACLES YOU FACE OR
MISTAKES YOU MAKE ALONG THE WAY; GOD WILL
HELP YOU FINISH YOUR RACE STRONG.

WHATEVER HE CALLS YOU TO DO, KNOW THAT
HE WILL HELP YOU DO IT.

NEVER GIVE UP ON YOU!
MAY YOU ALWAYS KNOW
YOU ARE HIS BELOVED AND
LIVE IN THE TRUTH OF ROMANS 8: 37 (AMP)

YOU ARE MORE THAN A CONQUEROR
THROUGH HIM WHO LOVED YOU SO MUCH
THAT HE DIED FOR YOU.

ALSO, TO MY FOREVER FAVORITE GIRL AND NUMBER ONE
SUPPORTER, MY MOM, DIARITA.

TO MY "BIG MA" LUCILLE MILLER,
MY LATE GRANDMA AMANDA,
AND GRACIE MAE,
WHO ARE FOREVER IN MY HEART,
TO "NANNY" FAITH AND JOHNIFER
MY "GRANDMA COMMITTEE",
AND ALL THE MANY PHENOMENAL WOMEN OF GOD
I HAVE BEEN SO PRIVILEGED TO HAVE IN MY LIFE.

TO MY SISTERS IN CHRIST WHO SPOKE AND POURED INTO MY
LIFE, ALL OF MY PASTORS, TEACHERS, CHURCH FAMILY,
EXTENDED FAMILY MEMBERS, AND FRIENDS —

EACH OF YOU WHO TOOK A PIECE OF MY BROKEN LITTLE HEART
AND HELPED MY HEAVENLY FATHER PIECE IT BACK TOGETHER
TO WHOLENESS, YOU ALL KNOW WHO YOU ARE AND I AM
EXTREMELY GRATEFUL.

LAST BUT NOT LEAST,
TO MY HUSBAND, DAEMAR AKA M.A.R.K.,
THANK YOU FOR BEING SO PATIENT WITH ME
AND LOVING ME THROUGHOUT ALL MY PROCESS.

A MOMENT OF PRAISE

You will keep me in perfect peace

Because my mind is stayed on thee

I don't have to run from the attacks of the enemy

Protected by your Armor, I will STAND strong

For I know Joy comes in the morning

And Trouble won't last long

So, I praise you Oh Lord, I lift up a Hallelujah to Your name

With your Spirit in me, I will NEVER be the same!

You said "No weapon formed against me would prosper."

One of the many promises of being YourBeloved Daughter

So, In the battle I will remember what my Daddy said,

Drawing my Sword, as I walk through the valley, I will forever lift my head,

Remembering, I am a child of the King, I don't know defeat,

My Trust is in you, the Lord God Almighty who cannot be beat

Isaiah 26:3
Ephesians 6: 10-19

Introduction

I remember praying a lot when I was a little girl. I may not have known a lot about how to do it "right," but I just started with where I was and what I loved to do. I would write letters to God about everything. That is also how I realized the poetic and prophetic aspects of some of my writings.

At times, some of my other pieces would be on current events or trends that I felt the need to address. I also noticed that each piece was based on scripture from the Bible. No matter how sad or down I was feeling, I felt encouraged by the time I reached the end of the poem! It was like I could never write one of those dark, deep, and gloomy pieces. I would start venting, but it would always end on a positive note.

I can see now that the Holy Spirit was leading me.
I remember when I felt Him telling me, "this isn't just for you." That is what started my journey to S.P.E.A.K. Life poetry and this book.

This is not your ordinary poetry book. S.P.E.A.K. Life VOL. 1 is a unique poetry book, devotional, and journal all in one. I want this to be more than just a collection of poetic literature and pieces. This is not just "*a* poetry book", it's *your poetry book*. You get to come along this journey and journal through its pages. You are invited to write your notes and/or stories and messages of hope, healing, and deliverance, and to speak life over yourself the entire way.

It is my hope that you won't leave this reading experience the same after you have read each piece. I hope and pray that this becomes one of your favorite poetry books/journals where you can explore and learn more about yourself and who you are in Jesus Christ as you grow stronger and deeper in your relationship with Him.

I pray that you, your Bible, and your S.P.E.A.K. Life poetry book, become best friends.

I wrote this book to:

- give and restore hope in you
- restore your sense of purpose
- and help you overcome the enemies of your God-given destiny, including anything keeping you from reaching your full potential in Christ.

This book represents so much to me. First, it represents grace and humility. I needed so much of God's grace and a good understanding of it to get this book done. It took me a while, but I told God as long as He would help me, I would keep pressing forward. It took a lot of unexpected twists and turns on the path to completion, but this book represents overcoming, resilience, and finishing despite the odds against you. This book also represents giving birth to the promise that nothing is impossible or too hard for God, and I mean nothing!

Writing this book helped me see God not only as Father but also as a loving, loyal friend. This journey has given me a new awareness and appreciation of His character and faithfulness.

Fear, anxiety, and confusion tried to come into my life and smother the passion for this dream/book/vision; But God was there patiently waiting and caring for me through every detail of the journey, bringing me reassurance and confirmation every time. He reminded me not to give up. He was there not only because He loved me but, because, you know what?

I still had a purpose to fulfill!

So do you!

He never left me and is the only reason
I am still here today! He is faithful to
His promises and His unfailing love for us.

Deuteronomy 31:6 says, *"Be strong and courageous. Do not be afraid or terrified because of them, for the Lord your God goes with you; He will never leave you nor forsake you."*

When He says in His Word that He will never leave or forsake you, that's what He means, *never*!! So, whether it be through words of encouragement just at the right time, or an on-time word through social media, The Lord knows how to get your attention and remind you of His love for you.

The question is, are you noticing and paying attention?

The theme of the first volume of this book is **Identity**.

I want to affirm and speak life into your identity as a beloved daughter of the Most High God.

Wow! Let's stop and think about that for a moment. The Lord God Almighty, the creator of the entire universe, "The" great "I AM" wants to call us *His daughters.*

He wanted an intimate, genuine relationship with us so much that He came down to die for us to be a part of His family forever. That's a really big Truth that I don't think we sit with long enough.

Have you ever stopped to think about how BIG, AWESOME, and *MAJESTIC* God is? Have you stopped to think about what it means for Him to be our Heavenly

Father once we receive His free gift of salvation? Don't worry - we will get to that a little later.

It amazes me every time I think of who He is and that He had a plan for us before we were even born.Often, your identity and purpose (the reason(s) God put you on this earth) go hand in hand. Knowing who you are in Christ and then knowing what He has sent and equipped you to do on this earth is necessary to walk in the power and victory that Jesus gave us.

I hope this book is a reminder for you never to lose sight of His purpose for you. I have found that knowing your purpose ignites a fire in you that can push you beyond any darkness in your life into the unspeakable joy of knowing Christ!

If you have not already, I want to encourage you to seek the Lord through prayer to know your purpose confidently. If you need help getting started, I got your back. *I am here for you!*

You can find a "Prayer for my Purpose" prayer on the Prayer of Salvation Page.

Please, know you are NOT here by accident!

You may have heard this a million times, but I want you to let it sink in. Whether planned or unplanned by your biological parents, you were a part of God's divine plan.

It may be hard to understand or sometimes comprehend with our natural minds, but that's when we use the mind of Christ and *live and operate by faith.*

Let's stop and talk about FAITH for a moment!

What is faith?

It is the foundation of everything we do as children of God! It is such an important concept and the very lifeline to our relationship with God.

According to Hebrews 11:1, Faith is the substance of things hoped for, the evidence of things not seen.

A Relationship with God Must Start with Faith

So as daughters of God, we must decide to be intentional in keeping a mindset, heart, and lifestyle of faith. We must protect our hearts from fear, which is the enemy of faith.

One quick way to stay in faith is to remember this very powerful and catchy acronym I heard Pastor David Cooper say in his sermon titled *"NO More Fear"* last year. He said to turn your fear into Faith by remembering that (Faith Expects Amazing Results)! Wow, good, right!

Hebrews 11:6 says, "But without faith, it is impossible to please Him, (God) for He who comes to God must first believe that He is and that He is a rewarder of those who diligently seek Him.

We seek God *by faith*!

We trust God *by Faith*!!

We worship and praise God *by Faith*!!

Trusting that He in His infinite wisdom knows best. As daughters and children of God, we do everything by faith, and we aim to be led by the Holy Spirit. We walk in our God-Given identities and purposes by faith. We are on this journey together. Keep in the forefront of your mind that the first thing you were created for is fellowship with God and a relationship with Him. It's not about "doing anything to earn His favor and love first. *He already loves us First.* (1 John 4:9)

Remember, it is your faith that pleases God.   It   blesses Him when we believe in Him.   Our purpose is to realize our identity in Him and know who we are through His eyes. You were created to bless God, glorify Him, be loved by Him, and be called His very own. Once you get settled in that, what you do for God will flow out of a pure heart and understanding of His love for you and others. This will produce a powerful impact that will truly bless and advance the Kingdom of God for generations to come.

Let's get back to the mission and purpose of this book. This book is a celebration of overcoming all the odds against you and giving birth to the promise that nothing is impossible or too hard for God. It took me a long time to complete putting this journal together, although I had already written many of the poems in this book years ago as a teenager. God began speaking to me at that time to start sharing my writings and publish a book.

I must admit, I did what I think many of us do, which is to diminish our gifts because of our lack of confidence or because we just don't see the value in them as God does.

How foolish of us to question God, right? We don't mean to, but when we hesitate or second guess ourselves when He has called us and qualified us, we are saying, "Uh-uh Lord, you don't know what you talking about."

So many time, I thought, *"uh-uh, nobody cares about poetry, or my poetry is not like this or like that"*. I was blinded by fear and pride. Pride, you say?? How could insecurity be a form of pride?

Something I learned from a sermon by Min. Andrew Wommack was that from a biblical standpoint, pride is thinking anything else about yourself other than what God says about you. If you think about it, even being insecure is just another way of putting you and your feelings above God's opinions of you. This is especially true if you are aware that God is the one who is calling you or giving you a desire to do something.

Your best option is to take your opinions out of the equation and go with the opinion of God, who created you and all mankind. As the elders used to say, He knows us best, "better than we know ourselves." Here is where trust also comes into play. Proverbs 3:5-7 says, *"Trust in the Lord with all your heart and lean not unto thy own understanding in all your ways acknowledge Him, and He will direct your paths. Be not wise in thine own eyes. Fear the Lord and depart from evil."*

"Be not wise in thine OWN eyes" stands out to me. God is the one with infinite wisdom. Being prideful is the opposite of trusting in the Lord; you can't do both. I have learned that it's always best to Trust God and His Words, more than any negative emotions or feelings I may have.

As I started to grow in confidence in Christ and my walk with the Lord, there were times I did try to step out and do what He was leading me to do the best I could at that time. I realized that doing it was a stretching of my faith in the process.

It has been a very long time since I first felt the calling to publish this book. So much of "life," as they say, happened between then and when I first stepped out of the boat in faith, and many times, I felt like I was sinking.

I have been back and forth in and out of the boat many times, *often with one leg in and one leg out.* One constant and consistent thing was Jesus's outstretched hand to save me every time I tried to get out and walk on that water. I was often tempted to think it was too late that I should quit. *"God probably wants somebody else to do it by now,"* I thought. The feelings of failure played with my mind regularly.

I disqualified myself many times, but God would remind me of you every time. That's right, YOU and my purpose. He would send someone with an encouraging word not to quit at just the right time, as only He could do. I could hear Him say, *"Somebody needs it, and I still want YOU to do it. It's not too late, and just like somebody pushed through for you, you have to push through for somebody else."*

My *WHY* just kept carrying me and pushing me. Even though it seemed like the book was delayed to me, it is still right on time for someone. I had many more lessons to learn, battles to fight, and more confidence to gain to publish it at just the right time, in Jesus' mighty name!

PRAYER OF SALVATION

IF YOU ARE NOT A DAUGHTER YET,
MEANING THAT YOU HAVE
NOT YET TAKEN THAT
STEP TO ASK JESUS TO
COME INTO YOUR HEART,
I WANT TO EXTEND THE
INVITATION TO YOU TO ACCEPT YOUR
SEAT AT THE TABLE.

KNOW THAT EVEN THOUGH
YOU ARE NOT PERFECT,

JESUS SAID YOU WERE WORTH IT.

HE WANTS YOU TO COME JUST THE WAY
YOU ARE. LET HIM DO THE
**FIXING, CLEANSING,
AND HEALING.**

YOU MAY HAVE TRIED TO
FIX YOUR LIFE ON YOUR OWN,
BUT KNOW THAT HIS ARMS
ARE WIDE OPEN, WAITING
FOR YOU TO COME AND
GET YOUR CROWN.

JOIN US ON THIS JOURNEY TO
UNDERSTANDING YOUR NEW IDENTITY
AS HIS BELOVED IN HIS FAMILY!

GOD LOVED YOU SO MUCH THAT HE
SENT HIS SON JESUS TO DIE FOR YOUR
SINS, TO MAKE THINGS RIGHT AGAIN.

IF YOU WOULD LIKE TO ACCEPT JESUS
INTO YOUR HEART, RIGHT NOW, YES,
RIGHT NOW -

ALL IT TAKES IS TO SINCERELY SAY THIS
PRAYER OUT LOUD:

"HEAVENLY FATHER, IN THE NAME OF JESUS,
I COME TO YOU REPENTING OF MY SINS,
ADMITTING I NEED TO BE BORN AGAIN.

WITHOUT YOU,
I AM A SINNER WHO DESERVED DEATH;
BUT WITH YOU, I AM MADE RIGHTEOUS.

I CONFESS THAT I NEED YOU, JESUS.
I ASK YOU TO COME INTO MY HEART,
BE MY LORD AND SAVIOR, AND MAKE ME NEW."

ROMANS 10:9 SAYS IF YOU OPENLY DECLARE
THAT JESUS IS LORD AND BELIEVE IN YOUR
HEART THAT GOD RAISED HIM FROM THE
DEAD, YOU WILL BE SAVED.

"I DECLARE NOW THAT I
BELIEVE IN MY HEART,
AND I CONFESS WITH MY MOUTH
THAT JESUS IS LORD
AND THAT YOU, FATHER RAISED
HIM FROM THE DEAD.

I RECEIVE MY GIFT OF SALVATION
RIGHT NOW BY FAITH.

I DECLARE I AM SAVED, SET FREE,
AND WHOLE.

IN JESUS' NAME I PRAY,
AMEN!"

IF you said that prayer and meant it,
you are now saved!
Welcome to the Family!

Though you may not feel changed, just know that All of Heaven, me, and the entire body of Christ are rejoicing with you! WE ARE HERE FOR YOU EVERY STEP OF THE WAY!

I WOULD LOVE TO HEAR FROM YOU!

EMAIL ME TO RECEIVE INFORMATION FOR YOUR NEXT STEPS.

lakanjalawrites@gmail.com

I will connect and direct you to a couple of ministries for new discipleship resources.

Today I choose Life, Today I choose Christ

Today I chose to believe I have been made right

Today I choose to see the light

Today I choose the Joy of the Lord

Today I choose to believe I will soar

Today I choose to believe in what I was made for

Today I am redeemed

Today I receive the promise that Greater is He that is within me

And that by His stripes I am healed

Through the Power of the Holy Spirit, I am sealed

It's a Done deal!

_____

SIGN YOUR NAME

Signed,

Eternally Grateful

PURPOSE PRAYER

Father, in the name of Jesus,
we thank you for the opportunity and privilege
we have to come to you in prayer.
We come in with thanksgiving and praise,
lifting up your precious Daughter (Your Name).

Your Word says in Jeremiah 29:11 that
You have good plans in store for her.

We know that it is Your will, that we find You when we seek
You, and when we come to You, You will answer us. IF we ask,
seek, and knock according to your will, the door will be opened.

Lord, we ask that you *clearly* reveal your
Divine purposes and plans for
(Your Name) and her life.

Lead her in your way of everlasting hope.
May she receive your
divine dreams and your visions for her life.

May she recognize and follow the leading
of the Holy Spirit inside her and
thirst to be filled by Him.

May she come to know and hear Your voice clearly, declaring
that You are her Shepherd, she is Your sheep, and she will follow
You, and the voice of a stranger she will not follow.

May she recognize when You are speaking to her heart Lord, to
lead her down your paths of righteousness for Your Name's sake.
In Jesus name, I pray Amen!

Psalms 23: 1-3
The Lord is my shepherd, I lack nothing.
He makes me lie down in green pastures,
He leads me beside quiet waters
He refreshes my soul.
He guides me along the right paths
for His Name's sake.

DECLARATIONS

"I (Your Name) believe, receive, and agree with
this prayer, In the Name of Jesus Christ!
Amen! It is so!

"I know the purpose, thoughts, and plans the
Lord has for me, and I will walk in the fullness
of all He has created and called me to be and do.

*"For I know the plans I have for you, declares the
LORD, plans for welfare and not for evil, to give you
a future and a hope."*
Jeremiah 29:11

Based on Isaiah 54:17,
I declare that no weapon formed against me
(or my purpose and destiny) shall prosper,
and every tongue that rises against me in
judgment, I condemn in the name of Jesus!"

Speak Life

poetry

S upernatural
P oetic
E xpressions of
A nointed
K nowledge

Proverbs 18:21

"Death and *life are in the power of the tongue,* and those who love it will eat its fruit."

What is S.P.E.A.K. Life?

It's a unique style of poetry inspired by the Holy Spirit.

S.P.E.A.K. (Supernatural Poetic Expressions of Anointed Knowledge) Life

Supernatural - For the sake of this book, I want to describe the term *"supernatural"* to mean that I believe the content is divinely inspired by my Heavenly Father, God, "downloading", as some might say into my Spirit and heart. It's God putting His "super" ability on my natural gift and ability. I would further describe the process as when I am writing; the words seem to drop in my spirit and flow out almost effortlessly. Sometimes, I can hear the completed lines and stanzas in my head before I can even get them down on paper. I am sure songwriters can relate to this process when writing music and constructing a song.

For the most part, it flows without having to do much thinking! So that's why I call it supernatural. Contrary to how secular culture may portray the word *"supernatural"* there really is nothing spooky about it.

Poetic/Prophetic - Because the messages flow out in a rhythm and rhyme inspired by Holy Scripture and prompted by the Holy Spirit, most of my poetry has a prophetic tone. Prophetic poetry speaks life into situations with a voice of faith that tends to call things that are not, as though they are. Prophetic poetry comes from a voice of hope that speaks of a future outcome and perspective that is in tune with the Word of God. His perspective is always uplifting and life-giving.

Expressions - the process of making known one's thoughts or feelings.

(Of)

Anointed - God-ordained or set apart by God.

Knowledge- Information and Imparted wisdom. The information given by God to empower you; a knowing (awareness of God) that comes from the fear of the Lord.

What is The Fear of the Lord, you might ask? Does God want me to fear Him or be afraid of Him like He is a grizzly bear or a dangerous animal?

OH NO, my sweet sister.

To fear the Lord, or to have the fear of the Lord, means to have reverential awe, respect, and reverence for Him.

It means having a mindset and heart that immediately acknowledges Him in all of His Glory, Majesty Power, and acknowledging the holiness and truth that He is. It means *humility*.

The fear of the Lord is an understanding of His presence that causes you to remind yourself that you are in the presence of the King of kings. It's acknowledging the essence of who God is in every moment of your life and making the adjustment to act accordingly.

The fear of the Lord should make you check your behavior to put your best foot forward. To make it plain, it's like you putting some respect on God's name like the rapper Birdman demanded for himself, LOL.

How much more worthy of respect is God? It's an attitude and approach to life that prioritizes God and His word. It doesn't mean that we are perfect, but it does mean that we are *intentional*.

The fear of the Lord is similar to when the WORD is released into a situation in your life through your pastor, a friend, or your favorite devotional; *you value it.* It's acknowledging that God almighty said that! THE KING has entered the building people!!!

Imagine those old movies. You see how much respect people had when the king entered the room (if he was a good king, that is). Your posture changed, right? That's the fear of the Lord! And that's what we want to **S.P.E.A.K. Life** into!

Let's recap that and sum up the 3 R's of the Fear of the Lord. We are to have:

> **1. Reverential Awe -** the dictionary defines the word awe as an overwhelming feeling of reverence, admiration, fear, etc., produced by that which is grand, sublime, extremely powerful, or the like: God is awesome
>
> **2. Respect -** this word is defined as -esteem for or a sense of the worth or excellence of a person, a personal quality or ability, or something considered as a manifestation of a personal quality or ability: God is worthy of our respect
>
> **3. Reverence -** this word is defined as a feeling or attitude of deep respect tinged with awe; veneration. (dictionary.com)

Proverbs 1:7 (NKJV)

"The fear of the Lord is the beginning of knowledge, but fools despise wisdom and instruction."

Proverbs 9:10 (NKJV)

"The fear of the Lord is the beginning of wisdom, And the knowledge of the Holy One is understanding.

Psalms 111:10 (NKJV)

"The fear of the Lord is the beginning of wisdom; A good understanding have all those who do His commandments. His praise endures forever."

Proverbs 14:27 (NKJV)

"The fear of the Lord is a fountain *of* life, to turn one away from *the* snares *of death."*

1 Peter 2:17

"Show respect for all people [treat them honorably], love the brotherhood [of believers], fear God, honor the king."

How I began to S.P.E.A.K. Life!

I can recall my love for poetry starting as early as the 3rd grade. I can remember the first time I heard the term Haiku and got the opportunity to create one for homework. Although I don't remember the piece I came up with, I fell in love with the art form ever since and began using poetry to journal and express my feelings.

My notebook and pen became my best friends. There was always something so intriguing to me about a blank sheet of paper and pen or pencil that would seem to draw me in *like a magnet*. I couldn't resist the urge to write and fill pages with my thoughts or doodles, as I loved to sketch words and draw as well. I still do.

I remember having a little red notebook of poetry that I kept and collected from elementary school up until close to high school. I always had plans to publish that little red poetry book one day, but it somehow got lost when we moved. I would write random poems, but most of the time, my pieces would come out like prayers to God about the things that I would be going through that happened to rhyme.

Writing is therapeutic. I know that to be true for me, personally. Another purpose of this book is to encourage those who share in this passion for writing poetry to write or journal to do it even more and continue in it. I hope to encourage you to find the courage to share your thoughts with others so that you can find the healing, peace, joy, and fulfillment that comes from sharing it not only for yourself but for those it was meant to encourage as well. God used poetry to help me cope with and heal from a lot of painful situations I was dealing with over the years.

One of the biggest ones was fatherlessness and the void and pain that the absence of a good father can bring.

This is why this first Volume is called **IDENTITY**.

A prosperous soul starts with you knowing who you are in Christ, and who else can affirm and build confidence in who you are like your Father? Your Father's job is to affirm your identity and point you to the most important part of you - the identity your Heavenly Father gave you.

Strong dads build a foundation of security that affirms a girl's value and worth. The absence of that leaves her doing things to cover up the feelings of abandonment, rejection, and hurt.

I learned very early on that **MY HEAVENLY** Father was always there for me when my earthly one couldn't be. I found out that the first step in the process of healing is forgiveness. I had to learn how to quickly forgive my biological dad, so I could truly begin to heal and move on with my life.

I want to include a piece in this introduction that I wrote to my biological dad; a piece that I wrote as a late teen that helped me to start my healing process.

DADDY'S GIRL

School "first days", graduation and birthdays
Mama was there but where were you?
I don't know guess you had something better to do
I never said anything, I always assumed you knew,
the hurt and pain your absence put me through
I never wanted to call you a deadbeat dad
I remember the few times you gave me all you had
A few dollars for some "school clothes" but now I've outgrown those
I am a young woman now
struggling with things like this college tuition
If you were here, I wouldn't be contemplating stripping,
Wait a minute, that's too real, am I tripping?
Thank you, Jesus, I never did get caught up in no for real pimpin
But I did try a little sippin, trying to fit in
Thank God I didn't pick up that bad habit besides,
I didn't really like the taste,
And I am glad I didn't choose that fast money route,
but it was only by His Amazing Grace!
In the clubs, thirsty for your love, and attention
I thank God for my mother but it's you I am missing
Raising a child should be a couple's decision
Don't get me wrong I thank God for a mother so dependable and
strong

But if you were here, I wouldn't need all these loans,
I have kept all this in for so long,
I wanted to let it all out yesterday on the phone
When we talked for the first time in years,
I could barely talk, too busy holding back tears
I didn't know what to say, I didn't want to make you mad
And even though I was hurt at the same time I was glad
It felt good just to hear your voice and to know you were alive
Besides, I hadn't had this much of your time since I was about
five
Though you weren't there I never really went without,
things just seemed a little harder to come about
I had to work harder and Mama did too
trying to make up for the things you didn't do
At times things got frustrating - well everything except dating
I can say none of my boyfriend's found you intimidating
(and that's really not a good thing)
But it's okay daddy we all make mistakes
I just asked the Lord to show me His grace
To heal my broken heart and teach me His way
I learned there were other things to focus on than not having
you there
I got into His word and learned the power of prayer
God told me to forgive you and go on my way
I put you in His hands and prayed you would be okay.

So, Daddy, I love you is all I want to say
I wrote all this just to let you know that all the past pain,
I let it go
I forgive you so that I can prosper and grow
Unforgiveness blocks the blessing, so let the blessing flow.

Is this poem speaking to you?
Let's talk about it.
What thoughts are coming to mind?

_____

_____

_____

_____

_____

_____

_____

_____

_____

_____

_____

_____

_____

_____

_____

_____

_____

_____

I wrote this poem years ago when I was a freshman in college. I felt a lot of stress and financial pressure, which caused me to blame my dad a lot, especially when times would get tough.

I was working, trying to make *my own* way, taking responsibility by doing all that *I* could do.

I thought that my dad owed me something because I felt like I had missed out on so much. Everything was all about my feelings when it came to the situation. I now see that I was being way more selfish than I could see at the time. *A victim mentality was robbing me.*

The more I started to give my relationship with my dad to the Lord - the more Jesus would show me my dad's side of the story and help me to change my perspective. The Lord gave me a view of his struggles. My dad was only 17 when my mom had me, which says a lot.

God began to give me compassion for my dad. I began to see that my father was still dealing with many issues and hurt from his past. My dad was doing the best he could.

I was the product of teenage pregnancy. No matter how society glorifies and glamorizes teenage pregnancy,   I know how challenging it is to thrive in that state. It's only by the grace of God that many children in those circumstances overcome the strenuous conditions into which they were born.

Disclaimer: I am referring to young girls who have said they intentionally want to get pregnant and are seriously trying to do so as a teen. We have to address and correct this destructive way of thinking.

We can't deny the influence of pop culture, reality TV, and TV shows that glamorize teen pregnancy.

There is nothing cute about the emotional stress and drain placed on the child and parents in these situations. This is due to the instability of having a child out of wedlock without commitment to help raise the child. When you add the immaturity of the parents, it's a recipe for disaster.

Most of the time, one parent, usually the mother, is left with a huge portion of the work involved in caring for the child. Nine out of ten times - the grandparents are left to pick up the slack.

Having a baby is a huge responsibility that should not be taken lightly. It was not God's design for children to have children, especially unwed children, but we thank God for His grace and mercy. Things happen, and God, in His goodness, still extends His unfailing love and life-changing grace to come heal any and all the brokenness in our lives. *Praise God!*

He specializes in turning our messes into His masterpieces. However, that doesn't mean we should set our goals to become parents at a young age. These are lives we are talking about. Thinking it's cute to get pregnant on purpose to get your boyfriend locked down is setting a trap of unnecessary pain and trouble for yourself.

Now, if you have found yourself sincerely in an accidental teenage pregnancy and you are afraid and contemplating abortion, I am begging and pleading with you - PLEASE don't do that.

Make the decision to choose life. Please know that there is always a blessing in choosing LIFE!!!

I know you may be scared, or maybe you just don't want the responsibility, but please know GOD is able to heal, redeem, and restore you, once you put your trust in Him.

You will see that He is Jehovah Jireh, the God who provides for His children. There is ALWAYS hope. Reach out to your local church. You can also find at the end of this chapter a list of trusted pregnancy resource ministries and organizations that I support and trust for help and prayer in making this life-altering decision. The child's life is absolutely worth the struggle, trust me. God can and will help you in your situation.

My mom was only 15 years old when she gave birth to me, and I thank God that she didn't abort me. As hard as it was for her, she chose to give my life an chance. And I am here today writing this book to you because of her decision!

God healed and restored my relationship with my biological dad. Today, we are closer than ever. I am grateful we could let go of the past, move forward, and build a better relationship on a better foundation for our family's legacy and future. Trust me, this was not an easy process. I had to intentionally forgive him, put ALL the pain I felt in God's hands, and leave it there!

He is a great-granddad to my three kids, and I am so grateful he is around.

Now - it did take prayer, *a lot of it!* I'm sure there were a lot of people praying because my daddy had that bad boy reputation - the type the elders used to say "ran the streets." There was a lot of pain, and it took multiple tries, cries, and poems, like the one I just shared above.

When the time came to face my dad and have real conversations, there was no anger or blame, just a little girl and a love for her daddy that would never go away!

If you can relate to this poem and struggle with forgiving your dad, your mom, or anybody who was supposed to protect you, but hurt you and you're ready to release them along with any unforgiveness, bitterness, or hatred you may be harboring in your heart - will you say this prayer with me?

Heavenly Father,

Please help me see how much You have forgiven me. As an act of my will, in faith, I release and choose to forgive (_____) right now in Jesus name.

I receive Your grace to help me surrender all of my pain to You and move forward in peace today.

I apologize for holding unforgiveness in my heart against anyone who has hurt me in my past.

Based on Your Word, which teaches me to pray for my enemies according to Matt. 5:44, I pray for Your peace and protection over those who I was holding unforgiveness against.

I pray they will come to know you as Lord and Savior if they do not already, and that (_____) grows closer to you.

In Jesus' Name, Amen!

Pregnancy Resource Ministries and Pro-Life Organizations

Care Net

https://www.care-net.org/

Focus on the Family

https://www.focusonthefamily.com/pro-life/

LIVE ACTION

https://www.liveaction.org/learn/resources/

"But now thus saith the Lord that created thee, O Jacob, and he that formed thee O' Israel, Fear Not: for I have redeemed thee, I have called thee by thy Name; thou art mine!"

Isaiah 43:1

Remember, GOD, the Creator of the Universe, the same God of Abraham, Isaac and Jacob, Daniel, David, the Way Maker, Miracle Worker, and Promise Keeper," calls YOU, His own DAUGHTER.

You are His and He knows your name.

hello
MY NAME IS

THE INTRODUCTION

My Name is Lakanjala
Not La-Can-Jolla,
not "what cha ma" call her
It's Lakanjala, The King's Daughter!

I love my name
Even if you can't pronounce it
I will embrace my name and never again denounce it

Like it or not, your name chose you,
Don't let society or anybody Determine
if you like you

"All my life" I had to fight
negative Stereotypes like Your name is "ghetto"
Excuse me! What makes a name "ghetto" anyway?
Oh! Because it begins with L-A.
Uh, okay? Right, that makes a lot of sense
(sarcastic tone noted)
Because I am so tired of these bougie
attitudes being promoted

Granted they were words spoken in envy
Often times out of the mouth of a so-called friend
I was just a child, didn't quite understand it back then
But maybe I didn't like my name
because it became
the source of the attack
The easiest thing to poke fun at
Right off the bat

The Introduction, your name is the way you
introduce yourself to the world, it's Your I.D.

You may think, it's just a name, it's not that deep!
But I see the enemy's plan was for me to not like me
The subtle seed of deception and self-rejection
An all-out assault on my confidence,
It was no coincidence
I had the evidence of a stolen identity

But the accuser, the THIEF, has been found guilty.
Jesus took the pain, took the shame,
and gave me His name
The name that's above every NAME
Hallelujah, I've been redeemed!
Call me Unashamed

I used to not like my name because it made me stand out.
Now, I love my name because it makes me stand out

"Allow me to re-introduce myself",
My Name is Lakanjala, Daughter of the Most High King
That makes me a Queen and blessed, like to the extreme
(Deut. 28:13)
Like Everything That I touch prospers and EXCELS
Like Microsoft, it is His WORD
That prevails.
It's His WORD that never fails

My name SUITS me because I am clothed in His majesty
And like my name implies, I am beautiful and unique
Truly one of a kind, you will rarely find a name like mine
He calls me more precious than a ruby
And yes! Even before I was in my mother's womb,
my Father knew me (Jeremiah 1:5)

I am the BELOVED, fashioned and created in
His image for His namesake (Gen. 1:27)
I found myself in Him and HE makes my name great!!!

"Usually, I am humble", this isn't intended to brag
but It's time to love on myself
It's ok, I got permission from my Dad
It's all in His glory and honor that I bask, (Rev. 4:11)
So Now that I have your attention,

What is your name, might I ask?

Do you know who you are?

Let's take some time to reflect and
evaluate your current thoughts and
feelings about yourself.
Be open and honest with yourself.

Looking back,
in what ways do you feel like your confidence and self-esteem was attacked?

What labels do you currently identify with i.e., Fat, Ugly Skinny, Pretty, Smart, Dumb, and why? What do dislike about yourself and why?

_____

_____

_____

_____

_____

_____

_____

_____

Is there anything you like about yourself, and why?

_____

_____

_____

_____

_____

_____

Do you see in what ways you have given more value to things that are not true, or even the opinions of others over God's opinion of you?

_____

_____

_____

_____

_____

_____

_____

_____

_____

_____

_____

_____

_____

_____

_____

_____

_____

Let's try rewriting the poem "Introduction" to speak life and affirm the seeds of Christ and His greatness in you!

Take some time to re-read the poem titled "the Introduction", This time replace my name with yours below:

My Name is (Insert your name here)

I love my name
(or whatever you don't like about yourself here)

I will embrace my name
(or whatever you mentioned above) **and not denounce it**

Like it or not, your (insert whatever you mentioned above) **is a part of you**

Don't let society or anybody Determine *if* you like you
You may think, it's just a name, or (insert what you
mentioned above here) it's not that deep
But I see the enemy's plan was for me to not like me

The subtle seed of deception and rejection
An all-out assault on my confidence
It was No coincidence
I had the evidence of a stolen identity
But the accuser, the THIEF, He has been found guilty
Jesus took my pain took the shame and
put respect on my name in His name

Hallelujah, I've been redeemed! Call me Unashamed

I used to not like my (insert what you
mentioned above here) because it made me stand out

Now I love my (what you mentioned above)
because it makes me stand out

"Allow me to re-introduce myself,
My Name is" (insert your name here)
Daughter of THE Most High King
That makes me a Queen and blessed, like to the extreme
(Deut. 28:13)
Like Everything that I touch prospers and EXCELS
Like Microsoft, it is His WORD that prevails.
It's His WORD that never fails

I am the BELOVED, fashioned created in His image
(Gen. 1:27), for His Namesake
I found myself in Him and HE makes my name great!!!

"Usually I am humble", and I don't mean to brag
but It's time to love myself
It's ok I got permission from my Dad
It's all in His glory and Honor that I bask (Rev. 4:11)
so, now that I have your attention,

What is your name might I ask?

In what ways will you combat those lies with the truth of God's word!?

_____

_____

_____

_____

_____

_____

_____

_____

_____

_____

_____

_____

_____

_____

_____

_____

Take note of how you're feeling
at this moment and describe
what you believe about yourself.

_____

_____

_____

_____

_____

_____

_____

_____

_____

_____

_____

_____

_____

_____

_____

_____

*Evaluate what has shaped how you
view and feel about yourself.*
Where do you think you got these feelings?
(Hollywood, social media, toxic relationships)

Now take your negative thoughts or beliefs about yourself and see if they line up with what's been revealed to you from the Father and His Word.

Once you identify that those feelings don't line up with what you have read and learned that God's word says about you. You can move to take action against them.

_____

_____

_____

_____

_____

_____

_____

_____

_____

_____

_____

_____

_____

Let's pray and cast down those lies and tear down any strongholds of doubt and fear that have tried to destroy your identity. Let's take authority over any ungodly hindrances to the prosperity of our hearts and souls right now in the mighty name of Jesus Christ.

Heavenly Father

I pray You give them a revelation of Your grace and LOVE for them. Father, give them an ability to discern and walk with the Holy Spirit, Who is the Spirit of Truth, like never before.

I ask according to Your will revealed In John 3:16 that says You loved us so much, You gave us Your Son Jesus, that whosoever believes in Him should not perish but have everlasting life.

I know that receiving Your love and walking in your Spirit of Truth is indeed the path to everlasting life. Thank You for leading this lovely one to their path of everlasting life in You today, Lord, In Jesus name we pray, Amen!

Faith Declaration:

When it comes to me and everything concerning me, I will think only of those things that are Good, lovely, and praise-worthy! (Philippians 4:8)

Now that we have spoken life over ourselves and evaluated any unhealthy views of ourselves,

Let's keep this process going by Daily Speaking God's Word over us through some daily affirmations.

Biblical
Affirmations
& Declarations

I am Forgiven!

1 JOHN 1:9 (KJV) 1 JOHN 2:12 (KJV)

"If we confess our sins, He is faithful and just to forgive us our sins and to cleanse us from all unrighteousness."

"I write unto you, little children because your sins are forgiven you for his name's sake."

I am Loved!

1 JOHN 4:16 (NLT) 1 THESSALONIANS 1:4 (NLT) DEUTERONOMY 23:5 (NLT) ROMANS 5:5 (NLT)

"We know how much God loves us, and we have put our trust in his love. God is love, and all who live in love live in God, and God lives in them."

"We know, dear brothers and sisters, that God loves you and has chosen you to be his own people."

"But the Lord your God refused to listen to Balaam. He turned the intended curse into a blessing because the Lord your God loves you."

"And this hope will not lead to disappointment. For we know how dearly God loves us, because He has given us the Holy Spirit to fill our hearts with his love."

I am Accepted!

JOHN 6:37

"All that the Father giveth me shall come to me; and him that cometh to me I will in no wise cast out."

I am Righteous!

2 CORINTHIANS 5:21

"For God made Christ, who never sinned, to be the offering for our sin, so that we could be made right with God through Christ. Made right with God, or in other words in right standing with God through Christ Jesus"

I am Redeemed!

GALATIANS 3:13, PSALM 107: 1-2

"Christ hath redeemed us from the curse of the law, being made a curse for us: for it is written, cursed is everyone that hangeth on a tree:"

"O give thanks unto the Lord, for He is good: for his mercy endureth forever. Let the redeemed of the Lord say so, whom He hath redeemed from the hand of the enemy"

I am Healed, Healthy and Whole!

MATT. 9:20-22

"And, behold, a woman, which was diseased with an issue of blood twelve years, came behind him, and touched the hem of his garment: For she said within herself, If I may but touch his garment, I shall be whole." But Jesus turned him about, and when He saw her, He said, Daughter, be of good comfort; thy faith hath made thee whole. And the woman was made whole from that hour.

Did you catch what Jesus said to her?

Your Faith in Jesus makes you God's Daughter, the WORLD says an outcast, but Jesus saw a Daughter!!

I am Delivered from Fear!

PSALMS 34:4, (AMP) 2 TIMOTHY 1:7 (KJV)

I sought the Lord [on the authority of His word], and
He answered me, and delivered me
from all my fears.

*"For God hath not given us the spirit of fear; but of
power, and of love, and of a sound mind.*

I am Wealthy!

DEUTERONOMY 8:18 (AMP)

*"But you shall remember [with profound respect] the Lord
your God, for it is He who is giving you power to make*

*wealth, that He may confirm His covenant which He swore
(solemnly promised) to your fathers, as it is this day."*

I am Victorious!

ROMANS 8:36–37 (KJV)

"Who shall ever separate us from the love of Christ? Will tribulation, or distress, or persecution, or famine, or nakedness, or danger, or sword? [36] *Just as it is written and forever remains written," "For Your sake we are put to death all day long;*

We are regarded as sheep for the slaughter."

Yet in all these things we are more than conquerors and gain an overwhelming victory through Him who loved us [so much that He died for us].

I am Able, Capable and Sufficient!

PHILIPPIANS 4:13 (KJV)

I can do all things through Christ who strengthens me

I am a Finisher!

PHILIPPIANS 1:6 (KJV)

And I am certain that God, who began the good work within you, will continue his work until it is finally finished on the day when Christ Jesus returns.

Just as God our Father is a finisher and is the author and the finisher of our faith. He finishes what He starts and accomplishes His will and plans and through His Holy Spirit's power in you, you will too!

HIDDEN TREASURE

Life can be

a beautiful Irony

You may have heard the saying, "we are all on a journey"

One where you have to lose yourself to find out

Your life is hidden with Christ

And that to truly live, you have to die,

Die to all the selfishness within

That's the significance of, "You must be born-again."

Sometimes losing "yourself" is when

you find Life's greatest treasures again

I'm talking about losing the "you" you worked so
hard to be in your own efforts,

The one based on your ideas of perfection,
yes that "you" that tired and burned out "you"

The "you" behind the facades you put up to run
from your insecurities

That's the "you," I am referring to

NOW Imagine losing yourself and finding your identity in someone else

Someone Extraordinary - the only person worthy of imitating

The one for whom you were created, the one who you were meant to be found and known by

You are His, He knows your name

REST in His arms again

Relax and Let yourself go!

Do this with me, inhale 1-2-3-

Exhale and breathe

Breathe in and receive

The "Breath of Life"

And His victory over all that has tried to weigh you down.

You were once lost, but now you are found!!!

The treasure is you, you are the hidden jewel

The pressures of life were only refining you

The treasure is the Word of God, too!

Hide it in your heart and bury it deep within.

That's the way you are guaranteed to win!

Matt. 11:28-29 *"Come unto me, all ye that labor and are heavy laden, and I will give you rest. Take my yoke upon you, and learn of me; for I am meek and lowly in heart: and ye shall find rest unto your souls."*

Is this piece speaking to you?

Are there any areas in your life where you have been trying to hold on to parts of yourself that are based on a fake image of perfection that you have been striving for? You don't have to strive for perfection anymore! Share your thoughts here and remember in Christ you already enough!

_____

_____

_____

_____

_____

_____

_____

_____

_____

_____

_____

_____

_____

_____

_____

_____

_____

_____

_____

_____

_____

_____

_____

_____

_____

_____

_____

_____

_____

_____

_____

_____

_____

_____

You Are
Royalty

"But ye are a chosen generation, a royal priesthood, a holy nation, a peculiar people; that ye should shew forth the praises of Him who hath called you out of darkness into His marvelous light."

1 Peter 2:9

You are royalty. YES, your Identity in Christ is regal- because we are joint-heirs with Christ Jesus.

Romans 8:17 *"Now if we are children, then we are heirs—heirs of God and co-heirs with Christ, if indeed we share in his sufferings in order that we may also share in his glory."*

What does that mean? What does that look like?

It looks like service and servanthood. It's a Kingdom mentality of humility and integrity!

Our Kingdom is powered by agape love. This type of love gives and serves others. Since we now know that our identity is Royalty. The goal is always to reign as Kings and Queens in this life - So Let's R.E.I.G.N.

R.E.I.G.N. means being
Rooted and
Established
In
God's
Nature of Love

"For this cause I bow my knees unto the Father of our Lord
Jesus Christ, of whom the whole family in Heaven and earth
is named, that He would grant you, according to the riches of
His glory, to be strengthened with might by His Spirit in the
inner man;

that Christ may dwell in your hearts by faith; that ye, being
rooted and grounded in love, may be able to comprehend with
all saints what is the breadth, and length, and depth, and
height;

and to know the love of Christ, which passeth knowledge, that
ye might be filled with all the fullness of God.

Ephesians 3: 14-19 (KJV)

We also see God's nature is love. God is love, *actually*.
1 Corinthians 13: 4-7-8 (AMP) describes God's nature:

"Love endures with patience and serenity, love is kind and thoughtful, and is not jealous or envious; love does not brag and is not proud or arrogant. It is not rude; it is not self-seeking; it is not provoked [nor overly sensitive and easily angered]; it does not take into account a wrong endured. It does not rejoice at injustice, but rejoices with the truth [when right and truth prevail].

Love bears all things [regardless of what comes], believes all things [looking for the best in each one], hopes all things [remaining steadfast during difficult times], endures all things [without weakening]. Love never fails [it never fades nor ends]."

"We have come to know [by personal observation and experience], and have believed [with deep, consistent faith] the love which God has for us. God is love, and the one who abides in love abides in God, and God abides continually in him."

1 John 4:16 (AMP)

In order to R.E.I.G.N. we must love others like God does! That means loving ourselves as God loves us, *too!*.

THE CORONATION

Beautiful Queen, are You Wearing Your Crown?

Or is yours somewhere in the lost and found?

Well, Jesus sent me to help search and rescue

I found a very precious one and I think it belongs to you

On this journey, know you're not alone,

I'm still adjusting to mine too

We have to get use to making His throne our home

Get used to the feeling that, there is where you belong

Get used to the fact that GOD calls you His very Own

I know sometimes you feel lost but I believe
He gave me these words to Remind you

That He said He would leave the 99

Just to find YOU

Don't fret or fear,
that enemy trying to bind you

In the darkest pit, Jesus is the Light that
will ALWAYS shine through

Leave all your worries, fears, and
mistakes behind you

He is the Solid Rock that can shatter
anything that binds you

Remember to not let anything but
His Truth define you!

He is the One who gives

Beauty for ashes

There is no greater Love that can outlast this!

Remember my dear,
not to be your own worst enemy

You don't have to search the world
looking for your Identity or validity

Through Christ! we are Daughters of the King and
that's enough

It means we may get knocked down sometimes

But we're tough

We don't give up and quit

We get up! Equipped!

To conquer, R.E.I.G.N., and rule by service in humility,
then we come back to pulls others through

That's what real queens are supposed to do

SISTER QUEENS

We all want the same things:
Love, respect and dignity
Our Queendoms should have
absolutely no room for envy

If I see your crown crooked, I'll help you fix it
If you think you don't "deserve" one,
it's my mission to help you get it
Yes! Sometimes we may think it's too big,
but dear Father, Help us fit it
Help us to admit it,
sometimes we need help to make better decisions

We all need each other, no more,
crabs in a barrel mentality
Let's make Unity in Christ our reality
The answer is to promote His LOVE like building
blocks-call us *Legos*
Let's go!! Building each other up to reach the top!

I think today's definition of queen
that is being defined by the TV and iPhone Screens
Has been sending the wrong message to
our young girls and teens

Like what makes us feel, valued, or Important,
and Powerful surely can't be all Materialistic But
do the young ones think having high morals and
standards is realistic?

When they are bombarded with fake Images
All made with cosmetic surgery better Known as plastic,
got millions of women making decisions so drastic
Messages so full of lies, stretching the truth so far, like
elastic
Enough of the evil tactics

We've seen a movement to stay woke and rightly so
Because the deception and slumber is serious, living
this life is no joke
But you can't fix something, when you
don't know it's broke

Let me correct my grammar, I know it's broken
Just like too many of these relationships,
we foolishly stayed in
It's beyond time to let the healing begin
But that's a side note, another rhyme for another time,
Let me get back to our current theme
Which is the definition of a Queen

When I say I won't judge you by your hair-do I won't
When I say I don't have anything against you I don't

Queens in His kingdom,
SERVE in integrity and humility wrapped in love because
we know who we belong to
Hating, gossiping, and slander is what we don't do
Sister Queens don't compete, we make sure we all eat!

"Sister Queens"

Sister Queens Coloring Page
Use this page to color in your own version of Sister Queens!

THE
Coronation
CONTINUED

ROYALTY DNA

When you're born a Queen
It's the King who validates your crown
So, sis you can stop looking around
When you know who you are,
people can't put you down
One thing is for sure His Kingdom
is big enough for more Queens to be found

I say found because the coronation is
a journey of self-discovery
It's your Identity recovery

To wear your crown proudly,
does take a degree of courage and bravery
It's not about a "look at me" mentality, it's one of
humility and a dependence On THE King's ability
It's about an unspoken/undeniable
confidence that a blind man could see
It's about a real purpose to set people free, that's
service to mankind

It doesn't matter what color is on the bottom of my
shoe If it's red, yellow, or blue
It's how thankful I am to wear them
It doesn't matter if I'm draped in diamonds and gold
too What matters is if I am willing to share them
or use them to

Take care of whomever has a need
as the Holy Spirit leads
It's about if I use these red bottoms
on my feet to share the Gospel of His PEACE Because a
real Queen knows -these things are temporal Real
Queens make moves for eternity!
A Queen is making sure things don't have you
But you have things to make an eternal impact
Giving in an abundance with no lack!
Being free to give, doing like Abba Father did

One of the most important things Jesus left us is the
legacy of Servanthood.
Which often seems most overlooked
Don't get it misunderstood
Yes, I believe we are supposed to prosper and Look good
But the heart of the matter is the matter of the heart

Real Queens keep their hearts protected
from the enemy's fiery darts
Keeping her shield of faith up at all times
She is loyal to the King and rules
her kingdom with Him always in mind.

ANOTHER MOMENT OF PRAISE

Lord, I Praise you and give you thanks for who
you are to me

You are the God of Peace,

You are more than what We need

You are the One who calms the raging sea

The rage in me, must flee, as I bow at your feet

Jesus Christ my King

The one who brings sanity to my calamity

the one who can do anything but fail

The one who is the Truth that I know will always prevail

Lord, thank you Jesus for removing the veil

My God, who has performed the impossible in my
midnight's

Lord you brought me back from the pit of depression
and gave me new life

Into my darkness You spoke life, you are my glorious
light!

You are my grace when I just can't get it right

You are my hope that with you one day, I know I will

You are my joy because by your Holy Spirit I am filled

You are my victory because by your stripes I am Healed

You showed me my purpose, when I felt worthless

Your loving kindness means everything to me

Your voice soothes my soul, fills my cup when it's empty,

Just one word

Is Everything

One Word from you is all we need

but you provided, a well, a fountain,

a river of living water flowing

for our thirst

I love you Lord but I am so grateful you loved me first,
even at my worst

So, at my least, I will give you my best

The least I can do is give you my yes!!!

The least I can do is a moment of praise

and turn this moment into the rest of my days!!!

You may wonder why I kept interjecting pieces titled "moments of Praise" throughout this book.

Psalms 22:3 *But thou art holy, O thou that inhabits the praises of Israel." Praise created an atmosphere where God could live with His people. It reminded them that He is Holy!*

Let's go a little deeper into what Praise really means. The dictionary defines it as:

praise/prāz/

> verb: Express warm approval or admiration of.:
> "We   can't praise Chris enough—he did a brilliant job".
>
> synonyms: commend, express approval of, express admiration for, applaud, pay tribute to, speak highly of, eulogize, compliment, congratulate, celebrate, sing the praises of, praise to the skies, rave about, go into raptures about, heap praise on, wax lyrical about, say nice things about, make much of, pat on the back, take one's hat off to, throw bouquets at, lionize, admire, hail, cheer, flatter, big someone/something up, ballyhoo, cry someone/something up, laud, panegyrize
>
> antonyms: criticize, condemn

noun: praise

plural noun: praises

noun: The expression of approval or admiration for someone or something.: "the audience was full of praise for the whole production".

synonyms: approval, acclaim, admiration, approbation, acclamation, plaudits, congratulations, commendation, applause, flattery, adulation, tribute, accolade, cheer, compliment, a pat on the back, eulogy, encomium, panegyric, ovation, bouquet, laurels, puffery, kudos, laudation, eulogium

Looking at the word praise in both parts of speech, we can see how deserving of our utmost, highest praise God is. Praise is inevitable when you embark on a journey that involves reflection of the hand of God and His goodness in your life.

You may be familiar with the phrase, "praise is a weapon". It's used to refer to praise as a source of spiritual power against the devil and his tactics against you. I do believe it is one of the weapons that Paul was talking about when he said that *"the weapons of our warfare are not carnal (worldly) but are mighty for the pulling down of strong holds* (2 Corinthians 10:4).

However, I want to focus on the power of praise and what it says to God and about your heart. *The more you take time to know and learn who you are and what you have been created to do, the more moments of praise become second nature when you are focused on the reality of who you are at the core.* Remember, you were created to worship, praise, and bring glory to your Heavenly Father.

We have a tendency to look back in regret from a negative perspective and get stuck. But sometimes God actually does want us to look back. However, it should only be if we can do so in a good way, as in evaluating where we have been and what He has done for us.

God reminded His chosen people on their journey through the wilderness to remember that He brought them out of Egypt. He reminded them that He was *their only* God. This was an opportunity for Praise and worship for them, but often they failed to remember who God was and what He had done for them.

When I think about God's goodness and all He has done for me, it awakens a praise inside my heart that I can't hold back. *When you praise God, confidence, peace, and joy come over you, making you feel invincible.* It changes the atmosphere. When you learn how to do this regardless of the circumstances, your faith muscles will really grow.

I want to share this particular piece entitled *The Ventilation of Veneration* to give honor and glory to God for all He is and has been in my life.

Sometimes we all just want to vent and let it all out. One way the word "vent" is defined in the dictionary is *"the expression or release of a strong emotion, energy, etc."* (www.merriam-webster.com/dictionary)

Let me encourage you my dear sisters, if you are going to "vent" let it be full of veneration (respect or awe inspired by the dignity, wisdom, dedication or talent of a person) for the King of kings.

If you are going to vent, let's be intentional to vent to the Lord first. He is the one who knows you best. *He is the only one who is 100% trustworthy, has your best interest at heart 100% of the time, and will never ever let you down.*

This is a great way to get to know Father God as your best friend and nurture your relationship with Him. Trust me lovely ones, seeking God first through prayer is always best and if you still desire someone physically to speak to ask Him to direct you to the right person to speak to in His way in His timing and watch how overcome with His peace and love you will be. He is a relational God, and it blesses and pleases Him when we come to Him.

He wants us to depend on and trust in Him, and I am so thankful for His love shown in this way.

THE VENTILATION OF VENERATION

I gotta vent and let this out!

Let the world know what this praise is all about!!

There's so much going on in the world,

let me get this off of my chest

The World is full of confusion, delusion and stress but one thing I know I am forever rocking with the best, That's J-e-s-u-s, Jesus Christ, He is the Word made flesh,

He loves you at your best

Even more at your worst,

He came to quench your thirst,

What manner of man is this? He gave up His life

He came to set you free, though you put up a fight

He stays by your side, in pursuit of your heart, day and night

Getting to know Him goes deeper than religion and traditions

It's sad to say but you can't see Jesus by looking at many of today's "Christians"

Gandhi called it out, I won't say they're all fake
Christians because sometimes it's just immaturity
and a lack of discipleship

I don't think, it means that their Salvation jumped ship,

However, I do apologize on behalf of all of us,
who at one time may have made "Christianity"
look bad,

Gandhi was fooled by the title's people had
not matching the fruit

We cannot be more concerned with
who we say we are and NOT accountable to
what we do!!

No more compromising the truth

If that has ever been you, please stop and repent!
No condemnation, no blame

We all have fallen short at some point and brought
shame to His name,

In the name of religion,
but Thank God for the gift of repentance

And freedom from the bondage of
man-made rules and traditions.

Trying to live with no flaws like
we could even come close to paying for it all

To ever be worthy of redemption without the Blood
of the Lamb and the authority in His name.

What a shame, Let's stop playing church,
we have no more time for games.

This time It's personal,

No more Religious walls, it's time to give Him your all,
Let His name be the only, one you call

Jesus Christ

He is the reason for breathing

He is soothing to my soul,
like a teething ring to a baby who is teething

He is like miracle grow to a hairline that's receding

He healed my pain, there is all power in His name

Just the touch of His garment is all We need

The power in His blood still redeems

It doesn't take much for a heart that believes

For the heart that receives

His Stripes healed all manner of sickness and diseases

Even Covid-19 -

There is nothing new under the sun

put all the viruses under the name of the Son

Remind the devil that the battles already been won

Jesus Christ, The GREAT M.D.

His blood is the remedy,
the transfusion that revitalizes me

His grace is the I.V. flowing life into me,
restoring my soul to His lifeline

My faith connects me to everything
I'll ever need in this lifetime

My prescriptions are filled with scriptures

My mind is filled with pictures

Of how He did it many years ago,

My Bible tells me so, it ain't no fables,

It's too late to convince me It's flawed, or otherwise

I recognize the lies!!! I ALREADY KNOW only Jesus
"Yeshua" is ABLE to save our souls.

He is Emmanuel "God with us," God wrapped in
Human Flesh.

I am a living witness, a testimony, living proof of His goodness. It was His amazing saving grace that I professed when my life was a mess.

It's too late to try to convince me He ain't the truth. I believe His Word is the infallible proof

When you feel like you been to the pit of hell and nobody but Jesus came through to save you

NOBODY can tell you He isn't the Truth… The Life and the only WAY

It's Personal this time and that's how it's going to stay!

It's those personal experiences and encounters with His Presence that go beyond words to express the feelings so fulfilling nothing can ever come close to duplicating.

So even when the world is out there advocating, plotting and thinking of eliminating our tangible source of connection to our Heavenly Father, His written WORD aka the Holy Bible,

You gotta hide it in your heart, where they can't even bother it

NO matter what they do or outlaw

It's so much deeper than religion, it's unfathomable - the depths of His love

That it was YOU He was thinking of

Imagine the lengths that Jesus was willing to go through to save little old me and you

Actually, He thinks You are a really big deal

So, let's take a moment to do some more work below↓ to heal.

Can you recognize God's Hand of grace and mercy and loving kindness in your life? If you are still standing here today and are reading this, I can guarantee you have some moments of praise of your own.

Let's take a moment to reflect back on tough situations you thought you would never make it through. Moments you know that it was no one *but* God who showed up for you in a major way. Whether it was big or small.

At the time, you thought it was drastic, but somehow you made it to this moment in time!

Look at how God's love and goodness has always been there for you.

My Personal Moments of Praise

_____

_____

_____

_____

_____

_____

_____

_____

_____

_____

_____

_____

_____

_____

_____

_____

_____

_____

_____

_____

_____

_____

_____

_____

HEALING THE GIRL BEHIND THE MAKE UP

We R.E.I.G.N. in all different shades

So, there is never a need to throw any
A queen has mastered being comfortable
in her own skin,
Whether she chooses afros,
weaves, wigs, perms, or dyes

Her Queendom is of substance, and what's inside
It's all about her WHY,

Like if you don't look like Kim K or Cardi B "
Do you look in the mirror and cry?

Or do you look in that mirror and
hold your head up high
Because you realize you have
more of a Brandy, kind of Vibe?

And that's absolutely fine because there is so much power
in realizing that she is just as beautiful too
The power is in knowing that God Almighty made YOU!

It's your RIGHT to choose what you believe
Beauty is for you-
Choosing what your REIGN will be about
Not holding on to beauty standards created by an
industry of fake Images and deception

If you feel like you are different,
embrace being the exception,
Be that beautiful exception to the norm,
Your Queendom is about knowing why you were born
Embrace that thing about you that makes you unique,
Change your perception of imperfections and your
definition of ugly or Flawed,
You don't have to live for other's applause

Change your view of rejection,
as they say it can be a way of God's Protection
There is BEAUTY in seeing and accepting YOU
in an unfiltered and pure State
And knowing that everything you are
made up of is great!!!

It doesn't mean you won't put the
makeup on or that wearing it is wrong
It just means that when you take it off, you're strong
And you won't flee, from the stranger you see
Real, raw, and Naturally pretty
Get familiar with that image
Get more comfortable with her

When you remove the makeup embrace her
Accept her, love her for who she is, allow her to be free
Allow her to be seen
Allow her to heal, to Feel
Allow her to reveal
The real you, beyond the insecurities
Beyond the issues that the makeup tries to hide
Let freedom inside
Don't reject them-Your imperfections, accept them

How did reading this poem make you feel?
Let's talk about it!

If doing this activity brought up memories too painful
for you to ponder, I want you to know that Father God
knows and He cares about those moments and feelings
you have.

Now would be a great time to confess those sore areas
and give them to your Heavenly Father to heal.

Psalms 147:3 says "He heals the brokenhearted and binds
up their wounds."

He wants to heal those wounds right now!

_____

_____

_____

_____

_____

_____

_____

_____

_____

_____

HEY MISS SOCIAL MEDIA!

Please Stop eating all the lies it's been feeding ya!
Stop feeling like you don't measure up
because you wear a B cup
Be Thankful, knowing that
what you already have is enough

Stop feeling like you don't make the cut
because you don't have a big injected butt Girl Stop!
You better embrace those skinny genes
Pull up those skinny jeans
And faith strut,
Shout out to Keilah J, my beautiful Sister Queen
We want you to know that
you are more than just a thing

You are the whole entire meal, nobody's side piece fling
You are worthy of that championship ring,
Worthy of a king, who is willing to work for it,
you don't want him to pay for it
You want a man that is willing to PRAY for it

Beloved, YOU ARE NOT AN OBJECT!
You are more than just a sight to see
You were Created to be more than a piece of meat,
But that's what we reduce ourselves down to when
we live by our natural desires'
Feelings and undisciplined flesh

Don't get your value from the size of your chest
Cover up a little more,
let your inner beauty shine through,
That's how you Attract God's best for you!

Please don't think this is from a
heart that's judgmental or cruel,
This is not about throwing stones at you
How dare I when I know my sins were too many! But
this is all about speaking the truth in love,
And helping you out the mess His grace got me out
of!

B.E.A.U.T.Y. FOR ASHES

"Truthfully, I think I'm ugly"
Girl!!!!!!!! Do you know how truly beautiful you are?
Do you know that you are already God's superstar?
You were born, unique and wonderfully made
I really hate to see you feeling this way!

"I don't like who I am"
Do you know there is nobody on earth like you?
Nobody can do what God has sent you here to do
No matter the circumstances surrounding your life
You will always be beautiful and worthy in the eyes of
Christ

"If I could just be like her"
Listen, I know how tempting and enticing it is these days
To go with the "Gram" and do almost anything for fame
Maybe even do things that get you called out of your
name,

But don't get caught up in the competition in the world
Most of those women you see are really hurt little girls
Who never really had someone to show them the truth
And the Value of the Word of God
that I am implanting in you

There is something very special
and precious in you,
A call to be different
Be a leader In Christ Jesus, you are a Believer
That means you believe you can do what God says you
can, say goodbye to self-doubt
These words are written to help you come all the way out
Of any depression or sadness, you may feel.
You are valuable, important
and your life does matter for real!

God loves you so much
that's why you are still here today
It's not about how good you are or
how much you do or don't pray

God is the good Father,
full of compassion and patience
He isn't mad at you for making mistakes
and ready to send you to Hell.
No, He just wants you to
come to Him first when you fail,
He has love and grace waiting for you,
come in and repent with a sincere heart,
God is ready and willing to give you a new start.

Stop believing lies and say yes to His truth
I am living proof that He wants to
Bring Out the
Excellent
And
Unique
Traits in
You
And make you new!!!!

YOU Are BEAUTIFUL
There is Beauty in everything He made including
you!!!!

"He has made everything beautiful and appropriate in its time. He has also planted eternity [a sense of divine purpose] in the human heart [a mysterious longing which nothing under the sun can satisfy, except God]—yet man cannot find out (comprehend, grasp) what God has done (His overall plan) from the beginning to the end."

Ecclesiastes 3:11

Beauty Redefined:
What makes a person beautiful in your perspective?

_____

_____

_____

_____

_____

_____

_____

_____

_____

_____

_____

_____

_____

_____

_____

_____

_____

_____

_____

_____

_____

_____

Do you know what God thinks beauty is?

"Don't be concerned about the outward beauty of fancy hairstyles, expensive jewelry, or beautiful clothes.

You should clothe yourselves instead with the beauty that comes from within, the unfading beauty of a gentle and quiet spirit, which is so precious to God. This is how the holy women of old made themselves beautiful.

They put their trust in God and accepted the authority of their husbands."
1 Peter 3:3-5

Keep in mind, this is not saying we can't look good and glamorous! God knows us and how we feel about our fashion. I truly believe we should give attention to our outer appearance and represent God well. However, don't be concerned about the outward appearance to the point that you neglect the more important aspect of beauty, which is that gentle and quiet spirit. *The scripture says this is precious to God.*

Having a gentle and quiet spirit doesn't mean we shouldn't have a voice. It means that we are to let the Holy Spirit, who is known to be a gentle teacher and counselor, be our guide in our speech and all manner of conversation.

Being pushy overly loud and aggressive isn't being a blessing to anyone.

Ouch! I am still a work in progress on this one myself! But Paul's words found in Philippians 1:6 say, "*being confident of this very thing, that He who has begun a good work in you will complete it until the day of Jesus Christ*".

God is working on us and we'll get there!

In 2016, I felt the Lord leading me to officially and publicly renounce the sorority I pledged in college. It was a process that started almost immediately after I graduated in 2005 as I began to grow in my walk with the Lord! I felt a strong desire to let go and purge any idols in my life, anything holding first place in my heart other than Him.

Again, this volume is all about recognizing and affirming our Christ-centered Identities, and knowing who we are.
It's about aligning spirit, soul, and body with what the Word of God says. The more I sought the Lord about His will and way for my life, and the more I surrendered and emptied myself to Him - The Holy Spirit opened my eyes to realize what I had accepted as a substitute for real intimacy. "Pledging" into a sorority, in particular,
continued coming up. I began to see that *simply not participating in activities wasn't enough.*

"This is a lifetime commitment," was one of the phrases I remember mentioned when going through the initiation process that stood out and didn't sit well with me. At first, I saw pledging as just a phase.

I served the community and did good things, but at the end of the day - the letters on my back got the credit and glory instead of Jesus Christ and His Church. I wasn't ok with the level of ignorance I realized I was operating in.

I already had a sisterhood and the opportunity to serve and do good in the name of Jesus Christ in the body of Christ without having to pledge allegiance to what I believe is modern-day idol worship.

I know this sounds harsh, but I believe it is the truth.

A POWERFUL REFLECTION

Looking in the mirror, pretty girl, pretty girl

What do you see?

That I didn't need a sorority to define me

Or to validate my "pretty"

Representin' 20 pearls, a disguise for the hurt I felt inside,

Truly lost and broken, strutting in survival mode

Longing for three Greek letters to try to hide the
holes in my soul

Fake attempts to be made whole

You'll be fine was the story I told

Myself to keep going through so I wouldn't really feel or
really didn't want to deal with the real issues that needed
to be healed

Just keep strutting in those high heels and caked up
makeup until one day you realize you struggle to want to
wake up
Wait this is way too deep

How did this pit of depression find me?

I thought it was just exhaustion or laziness
from being a stay at home wife and mom of
three and all that could very well be

But somewhere I had lost sight of my own true
identity. I had built a rocky foundation other
people's opinion of me

Deep down, truth be told, I needed freedom
 from the idol worship and strongholds

I wish someone had told me I didn't have to pledge to fit
in

That I didn't have to "pledge" to win

That I didn't have to "pledge" to be
comfortable in my own skin

But the skin I put on didn't belong to me, it
belonged to someone I was trying to be

Had I only known I didn't need a sorority to define ME

Following a false perception of perfection

Thinking my VALUE is in my connections

Or how pristine I was dressing

Or even what fine man I was (2 am) texting

um um um, I shake my head at the deception

It was real, I am putting it out there so someone else can
heal

I am putting it out there because obedience is key

I am putting it out there because I am glad Jesus delivered
me, truly set me free

That was not the person I found the more I looked in the mirror

The longing and thirst for acceptance and prestige many times led to compromise

I wish I understood that I was already accepted and loved in my Daddy's eyes

He gave me the mirror so I could see clearer

The Bible is the mirror, in case you didn't see the connection, look in it and see your reflection

I had to look in with new eyes filled with faith and a new heart ready for love and believe that it is all of His love that I am worthy of

And that is enough˙

I wish that I had known that I didn't have to be anybody else
Now I know that NO weapon formed against me shall prosper even those I formed against myself!

Isaiah 54:17

My process and journey to officially come out included sending a notarized letter to the director of membership stating my decision and reasons for renouncing my membership. Once I took that step of faith, I found out that many others had already gone through this process and that there was a whole community of believers and disciples of Jesus Christ who felt like I did and decided to come out of it.

For more information about those communities, you can visit www.outfromamongthem.com.

I also received testimonies from those who went through a similar process of feeling called and drawn to come out, as well as many others saying that they almost pledged, but they just did not have PEACE with going through the process.

I am grateful that God's grace and mercy kept me and pursued me with unfailing love and conviction. I came to a point in my journey where it was time to grow in my faith and walk with Jesus. I needed a solid foundation of my identity in Christ. The sorority's place in my heart was too big and had become a label and an idol that I had to let go of; simply not participating in sorority activities wasn't enough.

I knew that God was calling me to full submission and surrendering, as well as to a new life, new seasons and to a new IDENTITY in Him, one that is secure because He is the center of it.

As disciples of Jesus, we should be willing to let go of anything that is keeping us from full surrender to Him in our hearts, *no matter what it is.*

If you understand soul ties, then you will understand what I mean and why it is necessary to repent and ask the Lord to purify and cleanse you, which is something only the blood of Jesus can do. If my testimony can help even one person find a genuine and fulfilling closer personal walk with Jesus Christ, I will be forever grateful for that one and believe my job is done.

If you would like more information on the process to renounce again you can visit the website mentioned above (www.outfromamongthem.com). If youwould like to see an interview that includes more details about my experience making the decision to come out Greek membership and hear my story of renouncing, you can visit my website www.speaklifepoetry.org or contact me by email lakanjalawrites@gmail.com

BE ENCOURAGED

You are GOOD enough
You are Adequate, Capable, Valuable, and Priceless
You are a Success, able to defeat stress,
The definition of Blessed!
Now Refuse to accept anything less
Use your mouth to do good
And your heart will do better
You are more than a Conqueror
You are a Trendsetter
You are Remarkable, Reliable, Righteous, and Wise
You don't listen to evil one and his lies
You recognize, deception in any disguise
You are Virtuous, Beautiful, Intelligent,
The answer, Indeed Heaven sent
An Asset to the world, a contribution to society
Your life and your purpose matters, your personality gives
the world variety

Go forth and Boldly BE you
Now, knowing that You are enough,
Let's Dream! How will you change the world today?
What's one thing you may feel inspired to do and achieve
that maybe you had given up on or shied away from?

Maybe it's a new idea or vision. Tell me about it!!! Then set and make some goals to go get it! You go girl, you got this!!!

And the LORD answered me, and said, Write the vision, and make it plain upon tables, that He may run that readeth it. For the vision is yet for an appointed time, but at the end it shall speak, and not lie: though it tarry, wait for it; because it will surely come, it will not tarry.

Habakkuk 2: 2-3 (KJV)

We have come to the end of this S.P.E.A.K. Life Volume 1. on *Identity*. As you can see, the overall theme was affirming who you are in Christ, royalty!

We have learned what it means to be His queen and to live as God's beloved knowing you have value, and a special purpose. *May you never forget you belong to God and have a place in His Kingdom as a beloved daughter.*

One of the most important attributes of a child of God is obedience to the leading of His Spirit. Romans 8:14 says, *"For as many as are led by the Spirit of God, they are the sons of God".*

I pray that wherever you are on your journey, that you walk in humility and submission to the Lord and His plans for your life. That's how you live a life of purpose, peace and joy. I truly hope you enjoyed the journey and your coronation!

Wear your crown with confidence and walk with your head high; Fully assured and confident that you are loved and accepted by God through Jesus Christ! By now, I hope you realize what that really means. If you forget at any time, know that your Bible and S.P.E.A.K. Life poetry journals are here to remind you.

If this book has encouraged and inspired you to write your own poetry or share more of it in any way, please reach out to let us know! We would love to hear from you! My team and I are creating a whole S.P.E.A.K. Life poetry community to support and encourage young poets and writers like you!

Either way, I pray that this book blesses your life and helps you grow stronger in your faith as you walk with Jesus Christ.

Peace, Blessings, and much love to you,
Lakanjala "Elle" Williams

A MOMENT OF PRAISE OUTRO

The next time things don't go your way

And you feel too frustrated even to Pray

Feeling like you go through the same
problems day after day

When your Victory seems so far away

Stop right there wherever you are,

At work, at school, even in your car

And give God a moment of Praise

Take your mind back to that Calvary Place

Stop and think on the Love He displayed

The hurt and the pain He embraced for your sake

Think about all that Jesus went through and the price He
paid

So, when you are having a bad day, you can call upon His
Name and Pray

Cast all of your cares away, consistently Stand firm in
Faith

And watch how things Change

When we take the time to give Him Thanks,
instead of complain

AUTHOR BIO

Lakanjala K. Williams, also known as "Elle," resides in Snellville. Ga with her husband and three children. A native of Huntsville, Alabama, she is an Author, S.p.e.a.k.er/Poet, Host, Creative Writer, Model, and Entrepreneur but the title she holds most dear is beloved Daughter of God. It is her passion to help other women and young girls discover their true identity in Christ and ownership of this title as His Daughter.

Knowing first-hand how it is to feel lost and insignificant, she has defied the odds stacked against her, from being the product of a teenage mother to battles with significant depression and anxiety. Lakanjala is truly an overcomer with strength, courage, and faith in God that radiates resilience and hope to all those around her.

She is a powerful, compassionate speaker and Woman of God with an authentic vulnerability that truly resonates and connects with her audience. Lakanjala is armed with an electrifying passion for ministry and sharing the Gospel of Jesus Christ.

Through S.P.E.A.K. Life Poetry, she is on a mission to encourage, empower and equip girls and young women throughout the world with a strong sense of identity and confidence. Ultimately, building stronger families and communities, speaking life, and spreading love of God one heart at a time.

Connect with Lakanjala
and S.P.E.A.K. Life Poetry!

www.SpeakLifePoetry.org

LakanjalaWrites@gmail.com